OUTBREAK!

COVID-19 PANDEMIC

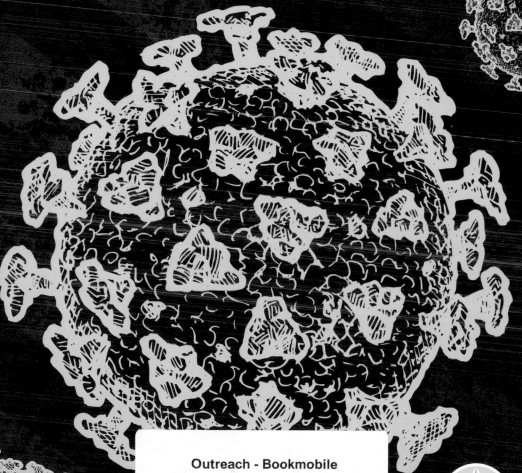

KENNY ABDO

Fly!
An Imprint of Abdo Zoom
abdobooks.com

abdobooks.com

Published by Abdo Zoom, a division of ABDO, P.O. Box 398166, Minneapolis, Minnesota 55439. Copyright © 2021 by Abdo Consulting Group, Inc. International copyrights reserved in all countries. No part of this book may be reproduced in any form without written permission from the publisher. Fly!™ is a trademark and logo of Abdo Zoom.

Printed in the United States of America, North Mankato, Minnesota.
102020
012021

Photo Credits: Alamy, AP Images, iStock, Science Source, Shutterstock
Production Contributors: Kenny Abdo, Jennie Forsberg, Grace Hansen
Design Contributors: Dorothy Toth, Neil Klinepier, Laura Graphenteen

Library of Congress Control Number: 2020911000

Publisher's Cataloging-in-Publication Data

Names: Abdo, Kenny, author.
Title: COVID-19 pandemic / by Kenny Abdo
Description: Minneapolis, Minnesota : Abdo Zoom, 2021 | Series: Outbreak! |
    Includes online resources and index.
Identifiers: ISBN 9781098223274 (lib. bdg.) | ISBN 9781098223977 (ebook) |
    ISBN 9781098224325 (Read-to-Me ebook)
Subjects: LCSH: COVID-19 (Disease)--Juvenile literature. | SARS (Disease)--Juvenile
    literature. | Epidemics--Juvenile literature. | Epidemics--History--Juvenile
    literature. | Plague--History--Juvenile literature.
Classification: DDC 614.49--dc23

TABLE OF CONTENTS

COVID-19

What began as a mystery to the scientific community, Coronavirus Disease 2019, or COVID-19, stopped the world in its tracks.

Though COVID-19 has not been around long, it may devastate the world for years to come.

SYMPTOMS

Typical **symptoms** of COVID-19 are fever, cough, and trouble breathing. Loss of taste and smell are other symptoms.

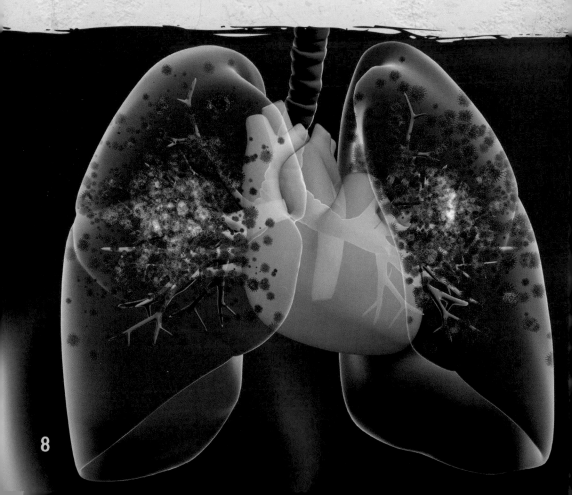

COVID-19 is deadlier for certain
people, like the elderly and those with
pre-existing conditions. People with
severe **symptoms** might go to the **ICU**
and need help to breathe.

SOURCE

1:18 PM   @ 100% ▪

🔍 🔒 coronavirus outbreak 2020

✕   ⊡ ⬆ 🔖

CORONAVIRUS
OUTBREAK

MGN

4:20
1 day ago

▶ Watch

YouTube
Coronavirus 2020 Coincidence Or Pattern?
1720 Plague, 1820 Cholera Outbreak &...

Uploaded by Sempornian Perspective, Jan 24, 2020

Coincidence Or Pattern? 1720 Plague, 1820 Cholera Outbreak &
1920 Bubonic Plague https://www.youtube.com/watch?
v=q06QWq1K1_c https://en.wikipedia.org/wiki/Gr...

Images may be subject to copyright. Learn More

Related images

COVID-19 is an illness caused by a certain coronavirus. All coronaviruses jump from animals to humans. Scientists believe COVID-19 can be traced back to bats that were eaten by humans.

When an infected person breathes, talks, sneezes, or coughs, they release tiny **droplets** into the air. These can land in the nose, mouth, or eyes of someone nearby.

OUTBREAK!

In December 2019, dozens of people suffered from **pneumonia** that came from an unknown cause. The cases were all linked back to the Wuhan **wet market** in China.

In January, a man from Washington state was confirmed the first COVID-19 case in the US. China put the 11 million people of Wuhan under **quarantine** two days later.

In March, the World Health Organization (WHO) labeled COVID-19 as a **pandemic**. **Quarantines** were put into place all over the world. The economy was put on hold. The stock market crashed.

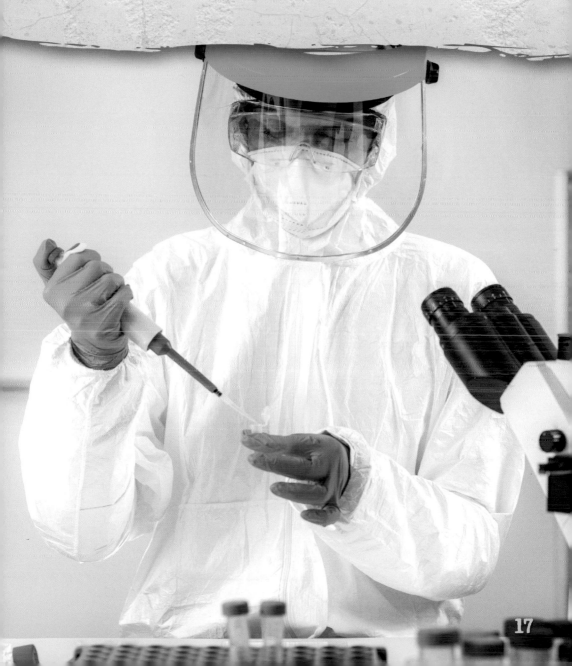

Scientists began work on a vaccine for SARS-CoV-2, the coronavirus that causes COVID-19. Early trials for the vaccine were promising.

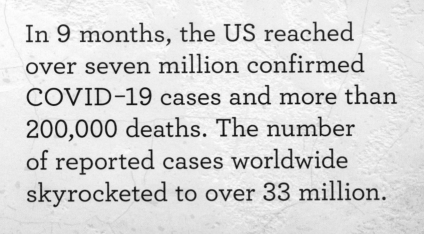

In 9 months, the US reached over seven million confirmed COVID-19 cases and more than 200,000 deaths. The number of reported cases worldwide skyrocketed to over 33 million.

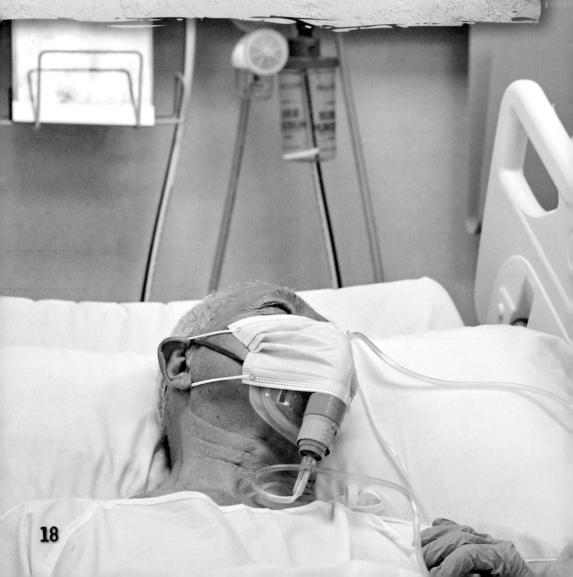

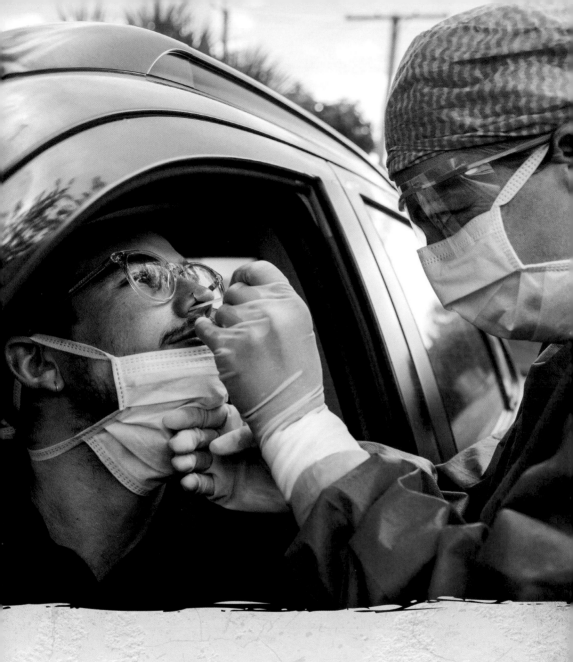

Scientists continue their work to understand and treat COVID-19. The more they learn, the faster they can defeat the virus.

The Centers for Disease Control (CDC) put out guidelines to reduce the spread of COVID-19. They suggest washing hands regularly, staying 6 feet (1.8 m) away from others, and wearing a mask in public.

GLOSSARY

droplets – produced when an infected person talks, coughs, or sneezes. Can spread a disease.

ICU – short for Intensive Care Unit, a special area in a hospital that provides care for the very ill and injured.

pandemic – a disease that spreads quickly around the world in a short amount of time.

pneumonia – a life-threatening infection that inflames both lungs and can fill them with fluid.

pre-existing – something that occurred from an earlier time.

quarantine – a period of time when sick people separate themselves from others to avoid spreading a disease.

symptoms – the signs that a person is ill or is becoming sick.

wet market – a place that sells fresh produce, meat, and fish.

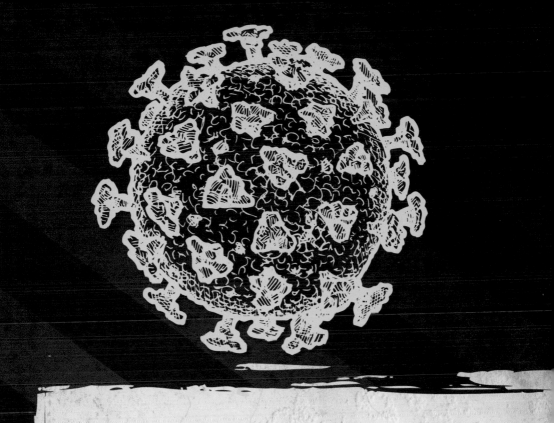

ONLINE RESOURCES

Booklinks
NONFICTION NETWORK
FREE! ONLINE NONFICTION RESOURCES

To learn more about COVID-19, please visit **abdobooklinks.com** or scan this QR code. These links are routinely monitored and updated to provide the most current information available.

INDEX